Exercises to Accompany

A Speaker's Guidebook

TEXT AND REFERENCE

Exercises to Accompany

A Speaker's Guidebook

TEXT AND REFERENCE
Second Edition

Dan O'Hair
Rob Stewart
Hannah Rubenstein

Prepared by
Melinda M. Villagran
University of Oklahoma

BEDFORD / ST. MARTIN'S
Boston • New York

Copyright © 2004 by Bedford/St. Martin's

All rights reserved.

Instructors who have adopted *A Speaker's Guidebook* as a textbook for a course are authorized to duplicate portions of this manual for their students.

Manufactured in the United States of America.

8 7 6 5 4
f e d c b a

For information, write: Bedford/St. Martin's, 75 Arlington Street, Boston, MA 02116   (617-399-4000)

ISBN: 0-312-40969-9

CONTENTS

CHAPTER 1—BECOMING A PUBLIC SPEAKER 1
    Summary Questions   1
    Short Writing Assignments   2
    Extension Activities   4

CHAPTER 2—GIVING IT A TRY: PREPARING YOUR FIRST SPEECH 5
    Summary Question   5
    Short Writing Assignment   6
    Extension Activity   7

CHAPTER 3—LISTENERS AND SPEAKERS 9
    Summary Questions   9
    Short Writing Assignments   10
    Extension Activity   11

CHAPTER 4—ETHICAL PUBLIC SPEAKING 13
    Summary Questions   13
    Short Writing Assignments   15
    Extension Activities   16

CHAPTER 5—MANAGING SPEECH ANXIETY 17
    Summary Questions   17
    Short Writing Assignments   18
    Extension Activities   20

CHAPTER 6—ANALYZING THE AUDIENCE 21
    Summary Questions   21
    Short Writing Assignments   22
    Extension Activities   23

CHAPTER 7—SELECTING A TOPIC AND PURPOSE 25
    Summary Questions   25
    Short Writing Assignments   26
    Extension Activities   27

CHAPTER 8—DEVELOPING SUPPORTING MATERIAL..........................29
    Summary Questions   29

    Short Writing Assignments   30

    Extension Activities   31

CHAPTER 9—LOCATING SUPPORTING MATERIAL..............................33
    Summary Questions   33

    Short Writing Assignments   34

    Extension Activities   35

CHAPTER 10—USING THE INTERNET TO SUPPORT YOUR SPEECH..............37
    Summary Questions   37

    Short Writing Assignments   38

    Extension Activities   39

CHAPTER 11—MAIN POINTS, SUPPORTING POINTS, AND TRANSITIONS........41
    Summary Questions   41

    Short Writing Assignments   42

    Extension Activities   43

CHAPTER 12—TYPES OF ORGANIZATIONAL ARRANGEMENTS...................45
    Summary Questions   45

    Short Writing Assignments   46

    Extension Activity   47

CHAPTER 13—TYPES OF OUTLINE FORMATS.................................49
    Summary Questions   49

    Short Writing Assignments   50

    Extension Activities   51

CHAPTER 14—DEVELOPING THE INTRODUCTION..........................53
    Summary Questions   53

    Short Writing Assignments   54

    Extension Activities   55

CHAPTER 15—DEVELOPING THE CONCLUSION............................57
    Summary Questions   57

    Short Writing Assignment   58

    Extension Activity   59

CHAPTER 16—USING LANGUAGE TO STYLE THE SPEECH ... 61

Summary Questions   61

Short Writing Assignments   63

Extension Activities   64

CHAPTER 17—METHODS OF DELIVERY ... 65

Summary Questions   65

Short Writing Assignments   66

Extension Activities   67

CHAPTER 18—THE VOICE IN DELIVERY ... 69

Summary Question   69

Short Writing Assignments   70

Extension Activity   71

CHAPTER 19—THE BODY IN DELIVERY ... 73

Summary Questions   73

Short Writing Assignments   74

Extension Activity   75

CHAPTER 20—USING PRESENTATION AIDS IN THE SPEECH ... 77

Summary Questions   77

Short Writing Assignments   78

Extension Activities   79

CHAPTER 21—DESIGNING PRESENTATION AIDS ... 81

Summary Questions   81

Short Writing Assignments   82

Extension Activity   83

CHAPTER 22—USING PRESENTATION SOFTWARE ... 85

Summary Questions   85

Short Writing Assignments   86

Extension Activities   87

CHAPTER 23—THE INFORMATIVE SPEECH ... 89

Summary Questions   89

Short Writing Assignments   91

Extension Activities   92

CHAPTER 24—THE PERSUASIVE SPEECH 93

    Summary Questions   93

    Short Writing Assignments   96

    Extension Activities   99

CHAPTER 25—DEVELOPING ARGUMENTS FOR THE PERSUASIVE SPEECH 101

    Summary Questions   101

    Short Writing Assignments   103

    Extension Activities   105

CHAPTER 26—ORGANIZING THE PERSUASIVE SPEECH 107

    Summary Questions   107

    Short Writing Assignments   109

    Extension Activities   110

CHAPTER 27—SPECIAL OCCASION SPEECHES 111

    Summary Questions   111

    Short Writing Assignments   112

    Extension Activities   113

CHAPTER 28—COMMUNICATING IN GROUPS 115

    Summary Questions   115

    Short Writing Assignments   116

    Extension Activities   117

CHAPTER 29—BUSINESS AND PROFESSIONAL PRESENTATIONS 119

    Summary Questions   119

    Short Writing Assignments   120

    Extension Activities   121

CHAPTER 30—SPEAKING IN OTHER COLLEGE COURSES 123

    Summary Questions   123

    Short Writing Assignments   124

    Extension Activities   125

NAME _____   DATE _____

CHAPTER 1—Becoming a Public Speaker

I. SUMMARY QUESTIONS

1. What are the similarities and differences between public speaking and other forms of communication?

2. How does public speaking benefit one's personal and professional development?

3. What are the elements of the public speaking process?

4. Why is it important for a public speaker to be culturally sensitive?

NAME _____   DATE _____

CHAPTER 1—Becoming a Public Speaker

II. SHORT WRITING ASSIGNMENTS

1. In what ways can effective public speaking benefit both your professional and personal lives?

2. Think of three speakers you consider effective. What makes them effective public speakers? In what ways do they influence the people around them?

CHAPTER 1—Becoming a Public Speaker

3. People such as Adolf Hitler and Saddam Hussein would certainly be identified as persuasive speakers. Do you believe they were/are effective? Why, or why not? What role does ethics play in judging whether someone is an effective speaker?

4. The thought of speaking in public arouses fear and anxiety in many people. Where do these feelings originate?

NAME _____ DATE _____

CHAPTER 1—Becoming a Public Speaker

III. EXTENSION ACTIVITIES

1. Talk to someone who works in a field that you are interested in. Ask the following questions: What specific communication skills are required in your line of work? How important are public speaking skills to your job?

2. Think of a conversation in which you tried to achieve a particular result (e.g., giving advice, persuading the listener). What are the similarities between that situation and public speaking?

3. List some examples of audience feedback, and identify each one as either positive or negative. When is positive feedback more appropriate than negative feedback? What are some ways in which speakers can deal with negative feedback?

4. Evaluate your own strengths and weaknesses as a speaker. What are three weaknesses that you want to work on during this course?

CHAPTER 2—Giving It a Try: Preparing Your First Speech

I. SUMMARY QUESTION

1. What are the steps involved in preparing a speech?

NAME _____ DATE _____

CHAPTER 2—Giving It a Try: Preparing Your First Speech

II. SHORT WRITING ASSIGNMENT

1. Why is it important to follow specific steps when constructing a speech? Why not just write whatever comes naturally?

NAME _____ DATE _____

CHAPTER 2—Giving It a Try: Preparing Your First Speech

III. EXTENSION ACTIVITY

1. After you have selected your speech topic, write a brief outline using the material from Chapter 5 as a guide. Remember to include a discussion of each step of the speech preparation. After you give your speech, refer back to the original outline and discuss how well you followed your plan.

NAME _____ DATE _____

CHAPTER 3—Listeners and Speakers

I. SUMMARY QUESTIONS

1. What is listening, and why is it important?

2. What is the relationship between listeners and speakers?

3. What are the major obstacles to active listening?

4. What steps can you take to become a more active listener?

5. What is critical thinking, and how does it relate to active listening?

6. What are some key points to consider when evaluating speeches?

NAME _____ DATE _____

CHAPTER 3—Listeners and Speakers

II. SHORT WRITING ASSIGNMENTS

1. Recall a situation in which listeners were rude. What occurred? What were the consequences?

2. How might rude listening manifest itself in the classroom?

3. What does it mean to be a "socially responsible" listener?

4. Do you believe that some people are "natural-born" listeners?

5. Name some famous people or some acquaintances who you believe to be good listeners. Explain why.

NAME _____ DATE _____

CHAPTER 3—Listeners and Speakers

III. EXTENSION ACTIVITY

1. Write five examples of speeches you saw on television or heard on the radio.

NAME _____ DATE _____

CHAPTER 4—Ethical Public Speaking

I. SUMMARY QUESTIONS

1. What is ethics?

2. What is the relationship between legal speech and ethical speech?

3. What is positive ethos?

4. According to research on speaker credibility, what speaker characteristics inspire trust?

5. What are values, and what is their relationship to ethics?

CHAPTER 4—Ethical Public Speaking

6. Why are awareness and appreciation of our own values and those of the audience important in ensuring ethical public speaking?

7. Name and describe the two characteristics that are universally seen as central to ethical behavior.

8. What other qualities do ethical speakers exhibit?

9. What is plagiarism, and why is it unethical?

10. How can you avoid plagiarizing?

NAME _____   DATE _____

CHAPTER 4—Ethical Public Speaking

II. SHORT WRITING ASSIGNMENTS

1. What advice about ethical public speaking would you give to a political candidate? Why do you think so many people are skeptical of politicians? Can you recall listening to any political speeches that struck you as ethically problematic? In what way?

2. Are profanity and vulgarity in public speeches unethical? Can you think of situations where they would seem appropriate? What types of situations, and why?

3. What should the penalty be for plagiarizing? Should the penalty for plagiarizing a work in its entirety be the same as that for plagiarizing only parts of it? Explain your position.

4. How can a speaker regain the confidence of those who have accused him or her of unethical communication?

NAME _____   DATE _____

CHAPTER 4—Ethical Public Speaking

III. EXTENSION ACTIVITIES

1. Listen to a speech on C-Span, or borrow a videotaped speech from your library. Does the speaker adhere to the criteria necessary for ethical speaking? Why, or why not? As a listener to this speech, what are your responsibilities?

2. Think about the times you have spoken in groups or at meetings. Was there ever an occasion when you could have been more ethical with your message? Explain.

3. Who are some of the most ethical people you have known? Have you tried to emulate them? What are some of the qualities you admired most about these people? Based on these qualities, what advice could you offer to others about behaving ethically?

4. Take another look at the checklist entitled "Identifying Values" on page 57 of the textbook. Choose the five most important values on the list; then select the values that are least important to you and to others. Now compare the lists of least and most important values, and explain why they differ. Do you think your values will change as you become more educated and gain more experience?

NAME _____ DATE _____

CHAPTER 5—Managing Speech Anxiety

I. SUMMARY QUESTIONS

1. What is public speaking anxiety (PSA)? What are some of the common fears associated with it?

2. When can PSA occur in the speechmaking process?

3. What are some consequences of PSA?

4. What strategies can you use to help you gain confidence as a public speaker?

NAME _____ DATE _____

CHAPTER 5—Managing Speech Anxiety

II. SHORT WRITING ASSIGNMENTS

1. Why is public speaking a source of anxiety for most people?

2. How can the adage "practice makes perfect" be applied to gaining confidence as a public speaker?

CHAPTER 5—Managing Speech Anxiety

3. In your experience, which strategies for gaining confidence as a speaker have been most helpful? Why?

4. Suppose a friend who has not taken a course in public speaking tells you that she has to give a presentation in one of her classes and is "scared to death." What would you tell her?

5. How can following the general procedures for planning a speech help a speaker become more confident?

NAME _____ DATE _____

CHAPTER 5—Managing Speech Anxiety

III. EXTENSION ACTIVITIES

1. List five experiences that give you significant anxiety. How does the anxiety you associate with these experiences compare with the level of public speaking anxiety you feel?

2. Describe occasions when you feel especially confident. What was it about yourself, the situation, or the tasks or other people involved that promoted your confidence?

NAME _____ DATE _____

CHAPTER 6—Analyzing the Audience

I. SUMMARY QUESTIONS

1. What are audience demographics, and what can they reveal about an audience?

2. What factors about an audience are important to know?

3. What are some methods of audience analysis?

4. Which features of the speech setting should be assessed as part of the audience analysis?

NAME _____ DATE _____

CHAPTER 6—Analyzing the Audience

II. SHORT WRITING ASSIGNMENTS

1. Why is it important to conduct a thorough audience analysis, even when a speaker will be giving a speech that he or she has given several times before?

2. Which would be most helpful in conducting an audience analysis of your classmates—interviews, surveys, printed material about them, or talks with others who have delivered speeches to them? Why?

3. Why would it matter that an audience is made up of more women than men, or more Asian Americans than Hispanics, or more argumentative than non-argumentative people? How would this information affect the way you choose to prepare for and deliver a speech?

4. What features of a speech setting are essential to consider in preparing a speech? Why?

NAME _____ DATE _____

CHAPTER 6—Analyzing the Audience

III. EXTENSION ACTIVITIES

1. Prepare a survey to use in conducting an audience analysis of your class. Include both closed-ended and open-ended questions to determine audience members' age, gender, socioeconomic status, ethnic or cultural background, and religious and political affiliation. Also include some questions that ask where listeners stand in terms of argumentativeness and receiver apprehension.

2. Consider the topic you plan to address in your next speech. Which factors in your audience-analysis survey are most pertinent to the development of your speech? Explain why these factors should be considered in planning the speech.

3. Make a list of questions based on your speech topic and purpose. Select five members of your class who represent a sample of the demographic and dispositional qualities obtained in your survey analysis. Interview these individuals. Decide which aspects of your topic seem most relevant and interesting to these people.

4. Consider the features of your classroom and the kinds of presentation equipment that are available. Write a brief proposal to the instructor suggesting improvements in facilities and equipment that would benefit audience receptivity to speeches in your classroom.

NAME _____ DATE _____

CHAPTER 7—Selecting a Topic and Purpose

I. SUMMARY QUESTIONS

1. What sources can a speaker use to select a topic?

2. What is brainstorming, and how is it used to generate ideas for topics?

3. What are the three kinds of general speech purposes?

4. What techniques can be used to narrow the topic?

5. How can a speaker clearly state a specific speech purpose?

6. What are some ways of composing effective thesis statements in support of your topic?

NAME _____   DATE _____

CHAPTER 7—Selecting a Topic and Purpose

II. SHORT WRITING ASSIGNMENTS

1. How would a different general purpose (e.g., to inform rather than persuade) change the way you would present a topic?

2. What is the difference between the specific purpose statement and the thesis statement?

3. What ethical considerations should you consider when selecting a topic and a speech purpose?

CHAPTER 7—Selecting a Topic and Purpose

III. EXTENSION ACTIVITIES

1. Using the word-association brainstorming technique, generate a list of fifteen to twenty topics that are suitable for an informative speech. Start with some of the following general topics and see where they lead you: hobbies, passions, campus issues, personal weaknesses.

2. Write five different thesis statements for five different topics. Be prepared to present your work to the class.

3. Describe the characteristics of an audience that affect topic selection (e.g., age, gender, religion). How do these affect the audience's response?

4. Conduct an online search using general keywords or topics. You can use bulletin boards and listservs on the Internet to browse topic ideas. After gathering ideas, work to narrow your search. Make notes about how you found topics on the Internet and how you narrowed your search along the way. Share your experiences with your classmates during class discussion.

NAME _____ DATE _____

CHAPTER 8—Developing Supporting Material

I. SUMMARY QUESTIONS

1. What supporting material should be used in speeches?

2. What is the purpose of a narrative, and when should you use it?

NAME _____ DATE _____

CHAPTER 8—Developing Supporting Material

II. SHORT WRITING ASSIGNMENTS

1. What features of a source contribute to its credibility? Is being famous a credible reason for being a source? Consider talk-show hosts. Are they credible experts on the topics discussed on their shows? What about their guests?

2. When you listen to a speech, how much supporting material do you expect to hear? What type of speeches require the most supporting material? Are some topics more dependent on support than others? Give some examples. Can a speech ever have too much supporting material? If so, when?

NAME _____   DATE _____

CHAPTER 8—Developing Supporting Material

III. EXTENSION ACTIVITIES

1. Make a list of data sources. Include both print and electronic sources (including those found on the Internet).

2. Make a list of sources that you think are unethical and/or not credible. Explain why they fall into this category.

CHAPTER 9—Locating Supporting Material

I. SUMMARY QUESTIONS

1. What is primary research? Where can you find good supporting material?

2. What is secondary research? Where can you find secondary sources?

3. How is supporting material critically evaluated?

NAME _____ DATE _____

CHAPTER 9—Locating Supporting Material

II. SHORT WRITING ASSIGNMENTS

1. What is the purpose of locating supporting material? Identify the two types of research that you can conduct to obtain this material.

2. How much time should you spend locating, analyzing, and organizing supporting material for a five- to seven-minute speech?

3. What factors should affect the construction of a timeline?

CHAPTER 9—Locating Supporting Material

III. EXTENSION ACTIVITIES

1. Find two examples of primary and secondary research used as supporting material in a magazine or a newspaper article.

2. Make a list of data sources, and then discuss how you might go about locating each source. Include both print and electronic sources.

NAME _____ DATE _____

CHAPTER 10—Using the Internet to Support Your Speech

I. SUMMARY QUESTIONS

1. What is the Internet? Why is it critical to understand how to use the Internet for research?

2. What is the difference between a search engine and a meta-search engine?

3. How can you critically evaluate Internet sources?

4. How can you give proper credit to sources?

NAME _____ DATE _____

CHAPTER 10—Using the Internet to Support Your Speech

II. SHORT WRITING ASSIGNMENTS

1. What is the purpose of locating supporting material on the Internet? What do you need to know in order to use the Internet for research?

2. What is the difference between a search engine and a subject directory? Give examples of each.

NAME _____ DATE _____

CHAPTER 10—Using the Internet to Support Your Speech

III. EXTENSION ACTIVITIES

1. Select a famous person from history or current events. Locate and print all the relevant information about the person you can find on the Internet. You should also record and evaluate the types of sources you find.

2. What search engines do you commonly use? How are they alike? How do they differ? How do you use them? (You may want to look at the table on pages 154–155 in the text.)

NAME _____ DATE _____

CHAPTER 11—Main Points, Supporting Points, and Transitions

I. SUMMARY QUESTIONS

1. What is the function of main points? How are they generated?

2. How can the specific purpose statement and the thesis statement help generate main points?

3. What is the function of supporting points?

4. What are transitions, and how are they used in a speech?

5. How do the principles of unity, coherence, and balance apply to the organization of a speech?

NAME _____ DATE _____

CHAPTER 11—Main Points, Supporting Points, and Transitions

II. SHORT WRITING ASSIGNMENTS

1. Why is it important for a speech to be organized in a coherent and meaningful way?

2. Why is it important for transition statements to be used in the body of a speech?

CHAPTER 11—Main Points, Supporting Points, and Transitions

III. EXTENSION ACTIVITIES

1. Assume that you have been asked to deliver a speech to incoming freshmen on the topic of social life at your college. Write a specific purpose statement that has three main points.

2. Your instructor will distribute fortune cookies. Write three main points for a speech on the topic of the fortune found in your cookie. Then develop fictitious evidence for supporting points to back up each main point.

NAME _____ DATE _____

CHAPTER 12—Types of Organizational Arrangements

I. SUMMARY QUESTIONS

1. What are the five main types of organizational patterns?

2. What are the differences between these patterns of organization?

NAME _____ DATE _____

CHAPTER 12—Types of Organizational Arrangements

II. SHORT WRITING ASSIGNMENTS

1. How does the choice of main points affect the organizational structure used to present a speech?

2. How does an audience analysis affect the choice of an organizational pattern?

CHAPTER 12—Types of Organizational Arrangements

III. EXTENSION ACTIVITY

1. Give an example of a topic that can be presented according to each of the following types of arrangement: (1) topical, (2) chronological, (3) geographical or spatial, (4) causal, (5) problem-solution.

CHAPTER 13—Types of Outline Formats

I. SUMMARY QUESTIONS

1. What are the five main types of outlines?

2. What are the differences between these types of outlines?

NAME _____ DATE _____

CHAPTER 13—Types of Outline Formats

II. SHORT WRITING ASSIGNMENTS

1. Among sentence, phrase, and key-word outlines, which is most conducive to effective speech delivery? Why?

2. As an audience member, how do you feel when the speaker reads an entire speech from notes?

NAME	DATE

CHAPTER 13—Types of Outline Formats

III. EXTENSION ACTIVITIES

1. Use the checklist on page 192 of the text to review the steps for creating a working outline.

2. Put your speaking outline on notecards. Give them to your instructor to review. Then, use your instructor's comments to make appropriate changes in the outline prior to giving the speech.

NAME _____ DATE _____

CHAPTER 14—Developing the Introduction

I. SUMMARY QUESTIONS

1. What are the functions of an introduction?

2. What are some effective ways to capture an audience's attention?

NAME _____ DATE _____

CHAPTER 14—Developing the Introduction

II. SHORT WRITING ASSIGNMENTS

1. Do you think most people listen to only the introduction of a speech and tune out the rest? If audiences tend to tune out the body of the speech, shouldn't the introduction be especially effective?

2. How can a speaker develop an introduction that will interest audience members enough to make them listen all the way through a speech? What clever strategies can you think of?

3. Think about the best introductions to television shows or movies that you have seen. What made these introductions so effective? Discuss as many features as you can think of. How can they be applied to a speech introduction?

CHAPTER 14—Developing the Introduction

III. EXTENSION ACTIVITIES

1. Write an introduction based on narratives or stories for each of the following topics:
   - drunk driving
   - illegal immigration
   - health care in the United States
   - financial aid for college students
   - a favorite vacation spot

2. Think of two of your hobbies or personal interests. If you were to write a speech about them, how would you build credibility in the introduction? Write statements that support your credibility for each.

CHAPTER 15—Developing the Conclusion

I. SUMMARY QUESTIONS

1. What is the function of a conclusion?

2. How does a speaker alert an audience that the speech is about to end?

3. Why is it important to challenge the audience to respond to the speech?

CHAPTER 15—Developing the Conclusion

II. SHORT WRITING ASSIGNMENT

1. To what extent does a speaker's personal style affect the type of conclusion he or she selects? Should serious people try a humorous conclusion, or should they stick with a quotation or a rhetorical question? Should individuals who have a keen sense of humor take advantage of it, or should they try a somber story or anecdote instead?

NAME _____ DATE _____

CHAPTER 15—Developing the Conclusion

III. EXTENSION ACTIVITY

1. Think of two current events or news stories. If you were to write a persuasive speech about them, how would you create an appropriate conclusion? List several ideas for a conclusion.

NAME _____ DATE _____

CHAPTER 16—Using Language to Style the Speech

I. SUMMARY QUESTIONS

1. Why is "writing for the ear" important, and what are some ways in which this can be accomplished?

2. How can you ensure that your language is culturally sensitive and unbiased?

3. Why is it important that speech language be simple and concise?

4. What is concrete language?

CHAPTER 16—Using Language to Style the Speech

5. How can you create vivid imagery in your speeches?

6. How can you use language to build credibility?

7. How can you use language to create a lasting impression?

CHAPTER 16—Using Language to Style the Speech

II. SHORT WRITING ASSIGNMENTS

1. Why is it important to consider the connotative meanings of words in appealing to an audience? How can an analysis of audience attitudes, values, and beliefs be used to evaluate the connotative implications of certain words?

2. Think of three or four instances in which you could incorporate slang, regional, or ethnic terms into a speech in a way that would be appropriate to the audience, occasion, and topic. Be ready to discuss these in class.

3. How skillful are you in selecting words that have just the meaning you seek? Many people use a printed thesaurus or one that is part of their word-processing package. For an excellent online thesaurus and dictionary, go to: http://humanities.uchicago.edu/forms_unrest/ROGET.html. Choose ten common words, and find a higher-level vocabulary equivalent for each.

NAME _____ DATE _____

CHAPTER 16—Using Language to Style the Speech

III. EXTENSION ACTIVITIES

1. Choose an object in the room around you. Without naming the object, write a paragraph describing it in detail. Read it to a classmate, and see if he or she can guess what the object is.

2. Review the paragraph written in Exercise 1, looking for metaphors, similes, and analogies. Have you created any? If not, try to describe the object using these figures of speech.

3. Select a piece of writing you have done—a speech, a term paper, or other work—and edit it. Can certain words and sentences be deleted to make the message clearer and more concise? Try using a thesaurus to substitute simple words for unwieldy ones.

NAME _____ DATE _____

CHAPTER 17—Methods of Delivery

I. SUMMARY QUESTIONS

1. What are the four general qualities of effective delivery?

2. What are the four methods of delivery?

3. Why is practicing the delivery important? What are some key points to remember when practicing a speech?

CHAPTER 17—Methods of Delivery

II. SHORT WRITING ASSIGNMENTS

1. In what ways is a speech like a conversation? What are some differences between conversations and speeches? What implications do these differences have for understanding speaker delivery?

2. Why is enthusiasm important to effective delivery? How might too much enthusiasm be detrimental to a speech?

CHAPTER 17—Methods of Delivery

III. EXTENSION ACTIVITIES

1. Observe yourself having a conversation. Recall how James Albert Winans likened a speech to a conversation. Note the ways in which your part in the conversation sounds and looks like giving a speech. How would you rate the quality of your composure, enthusiasm, and directness in the conversation? In what ways does the conversation feel "natural"? What similarities and differences do you see between your behavior in the conversation and your behavior in giving a speech?

2. Speaking extemporaneously occurs when a speaker delivers a prepared and practiced speech without memorizing it or reading from a text. With a partner, try to give one of the speeches you've already given in class.

NAME _____ DATE _____

CHAPTER 18—The Voice in Delivery

I. SUMMARY QUESTION

1. What are the elements of vocal delivery?

NAME _____ DATE _____

CHAPTER 18—The Voice in Delivery

II. SHORT WRITING ASSIGNMENTS

1. Can you think of speakers you've heard whose vocal delivery impressed you? What did you find appealing about their vocal quality? Consider pitch, rate, pauses, articulation, and pronunciation in your answer.

2. Because we tend to excuse people's articulation and pronunciation errors in conversations, why should we expect them to be more accurate in public speaking?

NAME	DATE

CHAPTER 18—The Voice in Delivery

III. EXTENSION ACTIVITY

1. Select a favorite passage from a novel, a play, a poem, or another piece of writing. Read the passage silently several times, trying to get a sense of what it means. Next, read the passage aloud into a tape recorder. Then listen to yourself reading the passage. Does your voice convey the meaning you think the writer intended? How accurate are your pronunciation and articulation? How would you assess your pitch, rate, and volume? Is every word clearly audible? Record another reading of the passage, this time trying to improve the way you convey its meaning. Listen again. Now, identify the strengths and weaknesses of your vocal delivery. How might these help or hinder your delivery of a speech?

NAME _____   DATE _____

CHAPTER 19—The Body in Delivery

I. SUMMARY QUESTIONS

1. What are the functions of nonverbal behavior in delivery?

2. How does the speaker's body language—face, eye, and body movements—affect the way the audience receives the spoken message?

3. Why is practicing the delivery important? What are some key points to remember when practicing your speech?

NAME _____ DATE _____

CHAPTER 19—The Body in Delivery

II. SHORT WRITING ASSIGNMENTS

1. Why is eye contact critical in effective delivery?

2. When selecting clothes to wear for your next speech, should comfort or appropriateness be your first consideration? Why?

NAME _____ DATE _____

CHAPTER 19—The Body in Delivery

III. EXTENSION ACTIVITY

1. Videotape yourself giving a speech. Evaluate your physical delivery: how natural, relaxed, enthusiastic, and direct is your nonverbal behavior? Pay particular attention to your facial expressions and eye contact, gestures and body movements, and your attire and use of objects. Which elements are used effectively, and how? Which elements are potentially distracting, and why? What could you do to overcome the distracting behaviors?

NAME _____ DATE _____

CHAPTER 20—Using Presentation Aids in the Speech

I. SUMMARY QUESTIONS

1. What are presentation aids? What role do they play in a speech?

2. What are some of the ways to present or display a presentation aid to the audience?

NAME _____ DATE _____

CHAPTER 20—Using Presentation Aids in the Speech

II. SHORT WRITING ASSIGNMENTS

1. Discuss the best way to use objects in presentations for audiences of one hundred or more. Make recommendations for small, medium, and large objects.

2. What types of speeches do not require presentation aids?

3. Discuss several ways in which visual aids can reduce speaker anxiety.

CHAPTER 20—Using Presentation Aids in the Speech

III. EXTENSION ACTIVITIES

1. Think about the last presentation you attended. Briefly describe the aids used in the presentation, and evaluate the speaker's choice of aids. Do you think these were good choices for the topic? What aids would you use for the same topic?

2. Suppose you were asked to give a twenty-minute presentation on differences in crime rates among major cities. Make a list of the presentation aids you would use. Next to each item, explain why you chose it. Would your choice of aids vary depending on your audience (i.e., a national meeting of law-enforcement agencies versus your classmates)?

3. Generate a short list of topics that would be likely to include the use of each of the following kinds of aids:
   - objects
   - graphs
   - diagrams
   - computer projection and display technology
   - slides
   - models

NAME _____ DATE _____

CHAPTER 21—Designing Presentation Aids

I. SUMMARY QUESTIONS

1. What should you consider when preparing an aid?

2. What are some tips for using color?

3. What are some guidelines for using words with visual aids?

CHAPTER 21—Designing Presentation Aids

II. SHORT WRITING ASSIGNMENTS

1. Discuss the tips for using typefaces, fonts, and sizes effectively.

2. What are your own personal challenges for preparing and using presentation aids?

NAME _____ DATE _____

CHAPTER 21—Designing Presentation Aids

III. EXTENSION ACTIVITY

1. Watch a video of sample speeches in which the speaker uses presentation aids. Write a brief description of the aids used. Could you read the type? Do you remember anything about the colors that were used? Do you think these aids were good choices for the topic? Which aids would you use for the same topic?

NAME _____ DATE _____

CHAPTER 22—Using Presentation Software

I. SUMMARY QUESTIONS

1. What are the benefits of presentation packages like Microsoft's PowerPoint?

2. What are the potential disadvantages of presentation software?

NAME _____ DATE _____

CHAPTER 22—Using Presentation Software

II. SHORT WRITING ASSIGNMENTS

1. What are some common mistakes speakers make when creating transitions and animation effects in PowerPoint slides?

2. Have you ever been at a presentation where the presenter used PowerPoint inappropriately? Describe what you most disliked about the presentation.

CHAPTER 22—Using Presentation Software

III. EXTENSION ACTIVITIES

1. Choose a fictitious presentation topic, and create a three-slide presentation. Either present the slides to the class, or turn them in on disk to be graded.

2. Ask a professor from another class to view an old slide show used in class. Give a brief report about the presentation based on what you have learned in this chapter.

NAME _____ DATE _____

CHAPTER 23—The Informative Speech

I. SUMMARY QUESTIONS

1. What is the goal of informative speaking?

2. What four strategies or approaches for defining information are available to the informative speaker?

3. How can a speaker help the audience comprehend the message?

NAME _____ DATE _____

CHAPTER 23—The Informative Speech

   4. What kinds of subject matter can be addressed in an informative speech?

   5. What are some key points to keep in mind while creating an informative speech?

NAME	DATE

CHAPTER 23—The Informative Speech

II. SHORT WRITING ASSIGNMENTS

1. What is the purpose of informative speaking? Is it difficult to present a purely informative speech—for example, one that does not reflect the biases of the speaker?

2. Do you think informative speaking lies in your future? If you have selected an academic major, relate it to situations in which you might give an informative speech. In what areas of your personal life might you be called upon to give an informative speech?

3. What can you do in an informative speech to help listeners understand and process your message?

CHAPTER 23—The Informative Speech

III. EXTENSION ACTIVITIES

1. Suppose you are asked to give a short, informative presentation about the Internet to a group of fourth-graders. Write a few paragraphs on message requirements for this presentation. What kind of organizational pattern will you use? How much technical information will you include? (Remember, children often know more about computers than adults do.) What can you do to be direct and clear in your explanation?

2. Practice using visualization and descriptive language. Think of an everyday object, such as a chair or a kind of food, and describe it in as many ways as possible.

3. Using the topic of welfare reform (an issue), how would you present the information to your classmates? What combination of definition, description, explanation, or demonstration would you select? What organizational pattern would you use?

NAME _____ DATE _____

CHAPTER 24—The Persuasive Speech

I. SUMMARY QUESTIONS

1. What is a persuasive speech, and how does it differ from an informative speech?

2. Under what four conditions should a speaker give a persuasive speech?

3. What key factors or principles, when heeded, will help your efforts at persuasion to succeed?

4. Classical rhetoricians such as Aristotle taught that a speaker could persuade an audience through three forms of rhetorical proof. What are they?

CHAPTER 24—The Persuasive Speech

5. How can the Expectancy-Outcome Values Theory model be used to change an audience's behavior?

6. How can the Elaboration Likelihood Model of persuasion be used to help audience members understand the speaker's message and modify their beliefs on an issue?

CHAPTER 24—The Persuasive Speech

7. How can the principles of speaker credibility be used to increase the persuasive appeal of a message?

CHAPTER 24—The Persuasive Speech

II. SHORT WRITING ASSIGNMENTS

1. What factors should you consider when using emotional appeals in persuasive speaking?

2. Explain in some detail the difference between a persuasive speech and an informative speech.

CHAPTER 24—The Persuasive Speech

3. Which do you think is most important to achieving persuasive outcomes in a speech: logos, pathos, or ethos? Why?

4. Name someone you consider to be a credible speaker. How much does the person's credibility depend on his or her message? How much does it depend on who he or she is as a person (e.g., character and trustworthiness, similarity to you)?

5. Describe a behavior common to your peers that could be the focus of change based on the Expectancy-Outcome Values model of persuasion. How can you apply the model to the behavior?

NAME _____ DATE _____

CHAPTER 24—The Persuasive Speech

6. Using the Elaboration Likelihood Model as a framework, what suggestions can you give your instructor that would help him or her enhance the class's understanding of persuasive speaking?

NAME	DATE

CHAPTER 24—The Persuasive Speech

III. EXTENSION ACTIVITIES

1. Select one of the sample speeches in the Sample Speech portion of the text (p. 457). Analyze the speech for its use of logos, pathos, and ethos. Identify places where the speech makes appeals to audience needs and attitudes, and state what behavior or set of actions (if any) the speaker wants the audience to engage in. Estimate how long you could pay attention to this speech without being distracted by the characteristics or qualities of the speaker. Note anything the speaker says that enhances the speaker-audience relationship; does it affect your perception of the speaker's expertise, trustworthiness, similarity, or attractiveness?

2. Analyze the same speech for its use of Maslow's hierarchy. Identify where different needs in the hierarchy are addressed in the speech, and comment on how effectively or ineffectively the speech addresses these needs.

NAME _____   DATE _____

CHAPTER 25—Developing Arguments for the Persuasive Speech

I. SUMMARY QUESTIONS

1. What is an argument, and what is its role in a persuasive speech?

2. What types of claims can be posed in a persuasive speech?

3. What types of evidence can be used in a persuasive speech?

4. What three tests of evidence can be used to evaluate the strength of a speaker's evidence?

CHAPTER 25—Developing Arguments for the Persuasive Speech

5. What various types of warrants can be used in a persuasive speech?

6. What is the inoculation effect, and why is it important to consider it in presenting arguments?

7. What are the fallacies that can weaken an argument?

NAME _____ DATE _____

CHAPTER 25—Developing Arguments for the Persuasive Speech

II. SHORT WRITING ASSIGNMENTS

1. Explain the difference between an argument and a verbal fight.

2. Which type of claim do you think is easiest to defend? Why?

3. If evidence supports a claim, why do we need warrants?

CHAPTER 25—Developing Arguments for the Persuasive Speech

4. In the ideal speech situation, on which order of evidence would you base your entire speech? Why?

5. Why avoid any of the fallacies of argument if using them can lead the audience to accept your claim?

NAME _____ DATE _____

CHAPTER 25—Developing Arguments for the Persuasive Speech

III. EXTENSION ACTIVITIES

1. Consider an upcoming speech you will be giving to your class. State one or more claims that are the basis for the speech. Identify the type of claim each one is. Identify a body of evidence you have access to that will support your claim. Provide a warrant for each piece of evidence that ties it to the claim. Are these warrants implicit, or will you need to state them outright when you deliver the speech? Why?

2. When you deliver your next speech, ask a classmate to identify any fallacies in your argument. Discuss each fallacy with your classmate, and determine why it was committed and how it can be avoided in the future.

NAME _____ DATE _____

CHAPTER 26—Organizing the Persuasive Speech

I. SUMMARY QUESTIONS

1. What are the three factors to consider when choosing an organizational pattern for a persuasive speech?

2. What organization would be best to use when facing a hostile or a critical and conflicted audience?

3. When addressing an uninformed, less educated, or apathetic audience, what two factors are more important than the way in which the speech is organized?

4. What pattern of arrangement is commonly used for persuasive speeches based on claims of policy and claims of fact?

107

CHAPTER 26—Organizing the Persuasive Speech

5. What are the steps in the problem-cause-solution pattern of arrangement?

6. What are the five steps in Monroe's motivated sequence pattern of arrangement?

7. Under what circumstances is the comparative advantage pattern of arrangement particularly effective?

8. What are the key elements in the refutation pattern of arrangement?

NAME _____ DATE _____

CHAPTER 26—Organizing the Persuasive Speech

II. SHORT WRITING ASSIGNMENTS

1. Which is most important to think about when you are choosing an organizational pattern for your speech: the nature of the arguments and evidence, the nature of your audience, or the nature of the speech purpose? Why?

2. How might a speaker build a strong claim of policy speech? What steps are contained in this organizational pattern?

3. Explain the difference between the comparative advantage pattern of speech organization and the refutation pattern of speech organization.

4. Could speakers use different organizational patterns in the same speech situation? Describe a real-world scenario in which this might happen.

CHAPTER 26—Organizing the Persuasive Speech

III. EXTENSION ACTIVITIES

1. Choose a topic that is a claim of fact, and then choose an organizational pattern that is appropriate to the topic. Explain in detail *why* you think the organizational pattern you have chosen would help you make your point in the best way possible in an actual speech.

2. Repeat the previous exercise for a claim of policy, and then for a claim of value. Is there one clearly superior organization pattern for each of your topics? Or are there several that you think would work equally well for certain topics? Why?

NAME	DATE

CHAPTER 27—Special Occasion Speeches

I. SUMMARY QUESTIONS

1. What is a special occasion speech, and what are its five broad functions?

2. What are the different types of special occasion speeches?

CHAPTER 27—Special Occasion Speeches

II. SHORT WRITING ASSIGNMENTS

1. What are some of the most noteworthy aspects of special occasion speeches that you have heard? Do poorly constructed and delivered special occasion speeches do more harm than good?

2. If you were asked to develop and deliver one of the special occasion speeches discussed in Chapter 27, which one would you choose? Which one do you find less appealing than the others? Why?

NAME _____ DATE _____

CHAPTER 27—Special Occasion Speeches

III. EXTENSION ACTIVITIES

1. Research three eulogies delivered by well-known individuals (see, for instance, *The Book of Eulogies* by P. Theroux). Do you see any commonality in their structures? What gives the eulogies power? Language usage? Personal stories?

2. Listen to a guest speaker on your campus. How does the introducer capture your attention and add to the credibility of the speaker? What are the strengths and weaknesses of the introducer's presentation?

| NAME _____ | DATE _____ |

CHAPTER 28—Communicating in Groups

I. SUMMARY QUESTIONS

1. What makes an effective group participant?

2. What makes an effective group leader?

3. How can a group go about reaching a solution to a problem or issue that it has been charged with solving?

4. What are five of the most common types of presentations delivered in the business and professional arena?

NAME _____ DATE _____

CHAPTER 28—Communicating in Groups

II. SHORT WRITING ASSIGNMENTS

1. Explain one of your own experiences as a member of a group, such as a committee, a campus club, a dormitory government, or a sorority. Describe the purpose of the group, the setting, and the other members. When making decisions, what roles did each of the members fulfill? Illustrate these roles with specific instances of behaviors or interactions.

2. What are some ways in which individuals who assume counterproductive roles in groups negatively affect the ability of the group to work together and make decisions?

3. Why is it important for a group to have a clear set of goals?

NAME _____ DATE _____

CHAPTER 28—Communicating in Groups

III. EXTENSION ACTIVITIES

1. Recall the elements of critical thinking from Chapter 3: evaluating evidence; analyzing assumptions and biases; assessing an argument's logic; resisting false assumptions, overgeneralizations, and either-or thinking; considering multiple perspectives; and summarizing and judging facts. How could using the elements of critical thinking make you a more effective group member?

2. How many times have you had the opportunity to serve as a group leader? How would you assess your leadership skills in these instances? Were you able to effectively set goals and encourage active participation among group members? If you have never served as a group leader, do you look forward to that opportunity? Why, or why not?

3. Recall a situation in which a group you were part of was guilty of groupthink. Did you go along with the group decision, even though you didn't agree with it, just to avoid conflict? Or did you pressure others to go along with the decision to keep them from voicing dissent? Analyzing the decision in retrospect, was it the right decision?

NAME _____ DATE _____

CHAPTER 29—Business and Professional Presentations

I. SUMMARY QUESTIONS

1. What is the difference between public speaking and presentational speaking?

2. What are five of the most common types of presentations delivered in the business and professional arena?

3. What styles of delivery are appropriate to business and professional presentations?

NAME _____ DATE _____

CHAPTER 29—Business and Professional Presentations

II. SHORT WRITING ASSIGNMENTS

1. How are preparing and practicing a group presentation similar to preparing and practicing a public speech? How are they different?

2. Why do the different kinds of business presentations use different styles of delivery? Why can't a speaker just use his or her preferred style of delivery for any kind of presentation?

CHAPTER 29—Business and Professional Presentations

III. EXTENSION ACTIVITIES

1. Consider the occupation you hope to have after receiving your college degree. Which kinds of presentations do you anticipate will be required in your job? Why?

2. Review the styles of delivery that are appropriate to business and professional presentations. Which style is most appropriate to the kind of presentation you just identified in Exercise 1? Why? Which style of delivery is most natural to you personally? Why? Do you see much discrepancy between your personal style and the style that might be required for presentations early in your career? If there is a discrepancy, what can you do to overcome it?

NAME _____ DATE _____

CHAPTER 30—Speaking in Other College Courses

I. SUMMARY QUESTIONS

1. What are some typical oral presentations used in college courses?

2. What are some typical audiences for these types of presentations?

CHAPTER 30—Speaking in Other College Courses

II. SHORT WRITING ASSIGNMENTS

1. Discuss the characteristics of effective presentations in science and mathematics courses.

2. How do arts-and-humanities presentations differ from other presentations?

CHAPTER 30—Speaking in Other College Courses

III. EXTENSION ACTIVITIES

1. Public speaking students often have experience giving presentations in other college courses. Conduct a panel discussion to explore your fellow students' thoughts on these presentations.

2. Suppose you are asked to give a twenty-minute presentation in a social science course. Write a brief outline of your presentation.